Dear Mary & ,
I am so [...]
thankful for your [...]
friendship through the years!
You both are treasured gems!
May you be encouraged through
Christ's love. You are continually
in my prayers.
Love,
Levena Hemmle
8/5/20

Dew Drops and Honeycomb

A Collection of Original Poems and Song Lyrics
Levena Hemmle

Dew Drops and Honeycomb

A Collection of Original Poems and Song Lyrics
Levena Hemmle

*As the dew of Hermon, and as the
dew that descended upon the mountains
of Zion; for there the LORD commanded
the blessing, even life for evermore."
Psalm 133:3*

*Pleasant words are as a honeycomb, sweet
To the soul, and health to the bones.
Proverbs 16:24*

TRILOGY

Dew Drops and Honeycomb

Trilogy Christian Publishers A Wholly Owned Subsidiary of Trinity Broadcasting Network

2442 Michelle Drive Tustin, CA 92780

Copyright © 2020 by Levena Hemmle

Rights Department, 2442 Michelle Drive, Tustin, CA 92780.

Trilogy Christian Publishing/TBN and colophon are trademarks of Trinity Broadcasting Network.

For information about special discounts for bulk purchases, please contact Trilogy Christian Publishing.

Trilogy Disclaimer: The views and content expressed in this book are those of the author and may not necessarily reflect the views and doctrine of Trilogy Christian Publishing or the Trinity Broadcasting Network.

Manufactured in the United States of America

10 9 8 7 6 5 4 3 2 1

Library of Congress Cataloging-in-Publication Data is available.

ISBN: 978-1-64773-271-4

E-ISBN: 978-1-64773-272-1

DEDICATION

This book is dedicated to my loving husband, Richard. He has been so supportive and helpful in so many ways. It is also dedicated to my children and their father, their spouses, my grandchildren, and my great-grandson. But all the glory and honor for any good or encouragement from this work go to my heavenly Father, my Lord and Savior, Jesus Christ, and the Holy Spirit, who used me only as a channel through which His Spirit flowed. I thank God for every experience both good and bad throughout the years that have influenced and fanned the creative sparks that birthed these poems and songs. Most of the lyrics included in this work also have musical scores which I would be happy to share upon request (dewdropsbook1@gmail.com).

CONTENTS

FOREWORD

We have had the privilege of knowing Levena Hemmle for many years. Her life speaks volumes of how God has been faithful to her. And she has willingly dedicated her life to serving Him and His people.

She is a genuine example of a godly woman who allows the gifts God has given her to flow freely to bless others. Her gift of writing will refresh your soul as you sit quietly and read the words that she has pinned. May you allow the Holy Spirit to speak to you through these beautiful poems.

Psalm 45:1: "Beautiful words stir my heart. I will recite a lovely poem about the King, for my tongue is like the pen of a skillful poet" (NLT).

Terrell and Tara Taylor
Lead Pastors of Live Free Church
www.livefreechurch.org

It is with great excitement for my friend of many years, Levena Hemmle, who is publishing her book of poems, that I write this endorsement. We were close friends as teenagers and sang together in our home church choir with Big Chief Jim Wetherington of the Statesmen Quartet. Levena is a gifted and talented woman of God and I look forward to reading the beauty of words she has penned from her heart. My husband and I worked in pastoral ministry during the same time as Levena and her late husband in addition to attending the same home church as teens and young adults.

Sandra Warren Roberts
Dahlonega, GA

As I read some of your writings, I could draw a picture in my mind of what you were saying. You certainly get the gift honestly from your family. I remember so well your Dad and Mom reading poems and original material they wrote. So glad my life was influenced by your family as I grew up in our awesome heritage. While on any journey I always look for opportunities to stop along the way to enjoy the scenery, a local meal or just something cool and refreshing to drink. The gift which God has clearly given Levena, enables her to capture your thoughts and take you to that peaceful place; that encouraging place; that spiritual mountain stream. As you read, "go there." Enter into God's presence and allow The Holy Spirit to speak through the pen of Levena Karr Hemmle directly into your heart. You will be refreshed!

Gary L Smith, Pastor,
Forward In Grace
Savannah, GA

Trust in the LORD with all thine heart; and lean not unto thine own understanding. In all thy ways, acknowledge him, and he shall direct thy path.
Proverbs 3:5–6

TRUSTING, LEANING, ACKNOWLEDGING

So often we hear or maybe even say,
"Don't tell me what to do. I'll do it my way!"
But so many times our way turns into a mess
And we have to admit His way was the best.

The transition from childhood to young adult
Is filled with these times of adolescent insult.
But in the long run after a period of time
They realize the ladder to maturity is hard to climb.

Our growth in God is much like the same
We falter and sometimes take His name in vain.
Forgetting to lean on His Word and love,

Yielding to the Holy Spirit—God's holy dove
When we come to crossroads in life and ponder
Should I go this way or go the way over yonder?
How can we know which is the right way to go?

Trust God, lean on His Word, He the way will show.
For in the trusting in Him and in the leaning
We are acknowledging His work has meaning
He will direct our path we should then follow
To fulfill the call for the task is hallowed.

Levena Karr Hemmle
March 2020

Cast thy bread upon the waters; for thou shall find it after many days.
Ecclesiastes 11:1

CAST YOUR BREAD

What do you have in your hand … only a portion of bread?
Bread that will sustain you for at least one more day?
You can hoard it and keep it just like you said,

Or you can share it with hungry souls who cannot pay.
And in the sharing, you open the portals of heaven
To multiply and cause the portion to grow
For when any gift from the heart is given
It becomes a seed of love that we sow.

You may not see the return from your planting
Seeds take time to take hold and germinate
But very soon you will see the ground breaking
And up pops a stem and leaves to their fate.

God has placed within each one of us
A seed of His love; how will we care for it?
Will we ignore or crush it under all our fuss,
Or will we nurture and keep it well and fit?

So after many days, it will return to us in bounty
A harvest of good fruit, love, and compassion.
How are you tending your seed God trustfully placed
In your life—be it talents, skills, or other passions.

Don't grow weary in the casting and sharing of your bread.
For in due season, the harvest will come like He said.
Just from that one little seed, comes an abundance
It's harvesttime, a time to rejoice, sing, and dance!

Levena Karr Hemmle
March 2020

But seek ye first the kingdom of God, and his righteousness; and all these things shall be added unto you.

Matthew 6:33

WHAT ARE YOUSEEKING?

What are you seeking, longing for within your heart and soul?
Riches, position or fame, honor, prestige, or power?
And if you get these things, their purpose will you also know?
To glorify, lift up yourself to the ivory tower?

Wealth and fame can vanish in a fleeting moment's time.
We can plan and think we know the future,
Have it mapped out down to the last dime.
But we can't see over the hill or around the next curve.

All prosperity and fame come from God, not man,
We may think we've done this, made our own way.
My friend, God holds your next breath in His hand,
And He's the One who lets us see another day.

He knows your heart's desires as well as your needs
And He's the One who brings it all about.
He's looking for hearts that will surrender, you see
To His will and way, that's what it's all about.

The greatest wealth you can have is to know you're His
For in Christ is the fullness of the heavenly Father.
Because of His righteousness, we can have all this
Love, joy, contentment, and a peace like no other.

Levena Karr Hemmle
March 2020

For if the blood of bulls and of goats, and the ashes of an heifer sprinkling the unclean sanctifieth to the purifying of the flesh: How much more shall the blood of Christ, who through the eternal Spirit offered himself without spot to God, purge your conscience from dead works to serve the living God?
Hebrews 9:13–14

NOTHING MORE

"There's nothing more we can do," the doctor quietly said.
Little did he know we know the Healer who bled
And shed His blood on dark Calvary's cross
So that we could know freedom and not suffer loss.

Freedom from sin and the great price we should pay
Freedom from sickness and disease died that day
Freedom to know we no longer need to dread
Where we will go when we are laid dead.

For Christ paid the price, His own precious blood
Bought healing as it poured out like a flood
Down to the foot of the old wooden cross
Where my sins lay, all my guilt now forever lost.

He gave His all, so that all could be saved
If only at the foot of the cross they've laid.
All their sins, guilt, and soul and body diseases
Covered now by Calvary's stream appeases.

Nothing more He could do but to give His all
Crucified, buried, and risen to the Father's call.
The Great Physician, the Healer, just call His name
Jesus, Risen Christ and Son of God, every day the same.

Levena Karr Hemmle
March 2020

To everything there is a season, and a time to every purpose under the heaven.
Ecclesiastes 3:1

SEASONS

Seasons come and seasons go
Some bring sun and others snow
Year after year we learn the signs
What they will usually leave behind.

Our lives are also lived in seasons,
Each one brings different reasons
To ponder, rejoice, or even shed tears
So many seasons throughout the years.

We rejoice at the birth of a new little baby
And picture them as a man or a lady.
Will he be strong and carry his own,
Or will he someday regret wild seeds sown?

Will she choose a career or become a mother?
Tending the house and caring for others?
Will they walk with God or go their own way?
What they will do is very hard to say.

But parents and teachers are given the task
To instill in them principles that will always last
And influence their choices and their decisions
In plotting the path that leads to their positions.

So I ask you, my friend, what season are you in?
Have you young ones you're training to send?
Have you shown them how to handle the season?
They may even now be pondering the reason.

Ask God to help you discern and know
Just what you need to tell them or show.
Through their seasons God will steadily guide.
He never fails. He'll always be right by their side.

Levena Karr Hemmle
March 2020

Dew Drops and Honeycomb | 19

Come, my people, enter thou into thy chambers, and shut thy doors about thee hide thyself as it were for a little moment, until the indignation be overpast.
Isaiah 26:20

Draw me, we will run after thee: the king hath brought me into his chambers: we will be glad and rejoice in thee, we will remember thy love more than wine: the upright love thee.
Song of Solomon 1:4

COME INTO THE KING'S CHAMBERS

O come into the King's chambers,
Bring your heartaches and your woes,
Come, and find rest and perfect peace,
All your troubles He already knows.

O come into the King's chambers,
There your every inner turmoil share,
Every disappointment unveiled to Him
For He longs to lavish His love and care.

O come into the King's chambers,
Perfect peace is waiting for you.
Lie at His feet in total surrender,
His healing balm your wounds to soothe.

O come into the King's chambers,
Find renewed life, purpose, and hope.
All is not lost in life's circumstances
He knows the struggles with which you cope.

O come into the King's chambers,
What joy awaits as He restores your mind,
Removes the anguish, fear, and doubts.
O what peace and contentment you'll find.

O come into the King's chambers,
Lavished by His love, bathed in His peace,
Vision restored by His healing touch,
Cleansed, renewed, all sorrow released.

O come into the King's chambers,
What reward surrender and waiting bring!
Where once was defeat and sorrow
A new song of victory you'll sing!

O come into the King's chambers,
Transformation is now complete.
New robes of joy, peace and love,
No longer robes of sadness and defeat.

O come into the King's chambers,
An extended hand of love outreached,
See the feast He has prepared for you,
Come, rejoice in His love, and eat.

Levena Karr Hemmle
2017

I thank my God upon every remembrance of you.
Philippians 1:3

I thank God, whom I serve from my forefathers with pure conscience,
that without ceasing I have remembrance of thee in my prayer night
and day; greatly desiring to see thee, being mindful of thy tears, that I
may be filled with joy; when I call to remembrance the unfeigned faith
that is in thee, which dwelt first in thy grandmother Lois, and they
mother Eunice; and I am persuaded that in thee also.
2 Timothy 1:3–5

DEAR HEARTS

As we travel through life, many faces cross our paths.
Many stay and become part of our lives in special ways,
While some are only for a brief period in time,
But are those who are special stay with us through our days.

Those who are special, see beyond our outward shell
And look deeper into our lives and get to know our heart.
We sometimes have to say good-bye to those friends,
Yet we know from our hearts they will never depart.

We remember all the fun times and warm memories
Shared through heartaches, tears, rejoicing, and laughter.
When we can't see them, be with them, or touch their hand
We recall those moments of hearty laughs and chatter.

Thank you, dear heart, for being one of my special friends
How blessed I am to have had my life touched by you,
So with this gift, you have a gift from my heart
Let it remind you of the beauty you have within you, too.

Levena Karr Hemmle
August 2019

"If the Son therefore shall make you free, ye shall be free indeed."
John 8:36 KJV

THE PRICE OF FREEDOM

"Freedom is not free"—it has been said—
To secure our liberties, we buried our dead.
Many have given their lives, paid the ultimate price
With their life's blood, they made the sacrifice.

The freedom to pursue life's highest dreams
Was stolen from many, or so it seems.
To American soil in bondage they came
Beaten, dehumanized, and in chains.

Forced to do their master's bidding
Or suffer the consequences unrelenting.
Some were blessed with masters kind and true
Who recognized they were God's creation, too.

Deliverance was the cry of those held fast in chains.
How long shall we suffer our bodies beaten and maimed?
Will the day ever come when liberty for all men is seen?
Freedom from a taskmaster so cruel and mean.

Finally, after years of abuse the day dawned
When freedom from slavery was finally won.
And once again they could pursue their dreams
Of a life free from bondage and screams.

A man named King sought the injustice to end
Champion of civil rights—he sought freedom for all men,

But another King fought the ultimate freedom cause
When He hung on a cross for the bound and the lost.
For God has created all mankind as His seed
Regardless of gender, race, color, or creed.
Each one an individual with their own uniqueness
Yet all a triune being after God's own likeness.

God's love does not draw boxes or lines
He loves us each individually, for we find
It's not that God is colorblind, you see,
He's a God who relishes and loves variety.

No two leaves, snowflakes, or humans are the same,
Yet He knows each one individually by name.
To Him, each is as precious as the other, you see,
Which is why He sent His Son,
Jesus, to be.

The ultimate price—for our freedom He came
To free us from sin's bondage and shame.
When we stand before God's holy throne,
He'll not see us by the color we're known.

For in His sight we're not known by a color
But by relationship—God's child, Jesus our brother.
He'll see us through the blood of His Son
For in His sight, we'll stand together as one.

Levena Karr Hemmle
January 2007

And the very God of peace sanctify you wholly; and I pray God your whole spirit and soul and body be preserved blameless unto the coming of our Lord Jesus Christ.
1 Thessalonians 1:23

GO WITH GOD AND WITH OUR BLESSING

Go with God and with our blessing,
Though our hearts are sad by your leaving.
We know God has a higher call and plan
And He holds you in the palm of His hand.

We thank God for all your labors of love
And pray His continued strength from above.
As you go to your new field of labor,
May His presence be to you a sweet savor.

As our faithful shepherd, you have served,
So receive our praise you so deserve.
And receive our love as you now depart,
For it comes from the depths of our heart.

A true man/woman of God, led by His Spirit
Your godly example, we'll not soon forget it.
For you lived the life before us all
Showing compassion for the great or small.

May God's loving hand lead and guide
And give protection wherever you abide;
And may His peace surround your family,
With abundant provision for every need.

Always know within your deepest soul
That your life made a difference to this fold.
Whenever you wonder if any worth you'll see,
Just remember the hearts you touched is the key.

Levena Karr Hemmle
October 2007

Blessed are the peacemakers; for they shall be called the children of God.
Matthew 5:9

BLESSED ARE THE PEACEMAKERS

God blesses those who work for peace,
For they shall be called God's children.
With so many who live in strife
Will you be one on whom He can depend?

To reach out to those who suffer
From the seemingly endless despair,
Every way they turn it's only trouble
And they wonder does anyone really care.

Whether they live or die, does it matter?
And so their lives are lost in depression.
Longing and searching for lasting peace,
Can anyone show them the Way and direction?

But there is One who can bring this peace
If only they will turn and look to Him
He who is the Prince of Everlasting Peace
The answer they seek, bring to them.

Jesus, the Prince of Peace, readily gives
This sweet peace to all who will call
On His name, from their doubts turn.
In Him find release from fears all.

Levena Karr Hemmle
March 2020

Study to show thyself approved unto God, a workman that needeth not to be ashamed, rightly dividing the word of truth.
2 Timothy 2:15

THE PASTOR'S STUDY

The pastor's study is a symbol of the calling of the Christian minister to be the shepherd of a flock of God.

Here sermons are prepared to feed the congregation on God's Holy Word.

Here the work of the Church is planned so that the congregation may grow in grace and bear fruit in fellowship, teaching, and witnessing.

Here you will always find a friend and counselor in time of need.

He will not be surprised at your sins,
nor will he judge you in them,
but he always invites you to share with him,
the wisdom and love of God,
the knowledge of forgiveness of sins,
and the saving grace of God in Christ Jesus,
our Lord.

You are always welcome.

Levena Karr Hemmle
June 2013

Then said I unto them, Ye see the distress that we are in, the gates thereof
are burned with fire: come, and let us build up the wall of Jerusalem,
that we be no more a reproach.
Nehemiah 3:17

DAY OF RESTORATION

This is the day of restoration
A rebuilding of broken walls.
The enemy sought devastation
And caused the tragic fall.

My heart and soul were lean
From years of neglect and abuse
No sign of growth could be seen
The Word lay closed, unused.

Barren, dusty, and spiritually dry
I longed for the refreshing rain.
When will He open the sky
And relieve the crippling pain?

From the inside out, then all around
The healing and strengthening must start.
Transformation can only be found
When to Him I surrender my heart.

Then the song of victory returned.
Reaching for my tools, joy on my face,
The trash from past defeats was burned,
Broken timbers and braces replaced.

With renewed strength and clearer vision
I begin the walls to rebuild.
Faith and grace brought provision
As mercy and love my soul filled.

Levena Karr Hemmle
March 2007

For this we say unto you by the word of the Lord, that we which are alive and remain unto the coming of the Lord shall not prevent them which are asleep. For the Lord himself shall descent from heaven with a shout, with the voice of the archangel, and with the trump of God: and the dead in Christ shall rise first: Then we which are alive and remain shall be caught together with them in the clouds, to meet the Lord in the air: and so shall we ever be with the Lord. Wherefore comfort one another with these words.
1 Thessalonians 4:15–18

NATURE TESTIFIES TO THE RESURRECTION

The death of a dear one is never pleasant to experience
No matter how many times it comes to us.
We question why and just can't make any sense,
Regardless of their age or health, it never does.

The little caterpillar crawls along the ground
Till the time he knows he must fall asleep
Wrapped tightly in his tomb cocoon so sound
Alone in the dark, the tomb his secret must keep.

After the appointed time of his life-changing sleep
He begins to stir, trying to free himself from his bond
Cracks begin to appear in his encasement deep
And new life, a leg, a wing, his work is soon done!

A beautiful butterfly emerges and flaps his wings
New strength and energy now flow through his veins
Before long he is totally free and begins to sing
No longer a ground dweller, no longer the same.

One day we, too, must fall asleep, encased in a tomb
But we know the One who has the ultimate power
To free us from death and the darkness that looms
He, too, experienced death, over us His life will shower.

As we rise from dark, damp tombs that held us fast
To meet Him like the butterfly in the air someday
Death can no longer threaten us, transformation at last
Our new bodies will rise in the air, never more to decay.

Levena Karr Hemmle
March 2020

I found him whom my soul loves.
Song of Solomon 3:4

MY HEART HAS FOUND A HOME

Who can quiet this longing in my heart?
Who can answer the questions and desire?
How long have I prayed for the time to start
When I could gaze into Your eyes of fire!

To once again feel the tender caress
Of the gentle touch of Your hand
And on Your arms of strength to rest
In Your wondrous love so grand.

Like a ship tossed about in stormy seas
My heart has wandered through the night
Looking for a safe harbor to appease
This broken, aching heart contrite.

Then like an angel so steady and calm
You walked into my lonely life
Over my heart spread Your healing balm
And calmed all the turmoil and strife.

Now my heart has found its home
A safe harbor of peace, joy, and rest.
No longer abandoned and all alone
For in Your love my heart is at its best.

Levena Karr Hemmle
August 2007

Dedicated to my husband, Rick

For God [our heavenly Father] so loved the world, that he gave his only Son;
that whosoever believeth in him should not perish, but have everlasting life.
John 3:16

MY FATHER'S LOVE

When I was just a little girl,
I'd climb up on your lap.
You'd open wide, your arms unfurled
Lean back, and take off your cap.

I needed to feel your arms of strength
My worries and fears to subside,
To sit and rest for time at length
Just feeling your love deep inside.

Your love guided me through the teen years
And into the years of womanhood.
As an adult, you'd comfort my fears
And encourage me like only you could.

The years have come and years have gone
No longer a little girl in size.
We both find ourselves now alone
Our spouses no longer by our side.

From heaven's portals they heard the call
And had to go be with Him above
But one thing that hasn't changed at all:
I still find comfort in your love.

You've been the perfect example
Of my heavenly Father's love.
Your patience and caring are just a sample
Of His everlasting love above.

Levena Karr Hemmle
February 2007

Dew Drops and Honeycomb | 33

For this reason a man shall leave his father and mother and be joined to his wife, and the two shall become one flesh.
Ephesians 5:31

ONE YEAR AGO

One year ago today, I became your wife
And together we started a brand-new life.
Though we were still relatively strangers
We knew in our hearts, there was no danger.

For our heavenly Father was in control
And we felt His peace down in our soul.
He gave us the assurance deep inside
That by each other's side we would always abide.

As the days and months of this first year
Have passed, you've only grown more dear.
I know without a shadow of a doubt
That His love has brought this all about.

For our souls have become as one
As we live and move in His Son.
True soul mates for all eternity,
That's how long my love will be.

Levena Karr Hemmle
March 2009

And when he had sent the multitudes away, he went up into a mountain apart to pray: and when the evening was come, he was there alone
Matthew 14:23

A PLACE OF QUIET SOLITUDE

There is a place you love to go
When life's cares get too hard to bear,
To get alone with God above,
A place your family shares.

Just a short drive and then a hike,
It's really not too far away,
But, oh, the difference it makes,
Just to go there for the day.

Cheaha Mountain is special, indeed
Good memories of Dad and Mom.
Though they are gone for now,
Yet they still bid you come.

Come to this place of solitude
Come, sit here alone and talk,
For they and God hear your prayers,
While there sitting on Bald Rock.

We hope you find this little gift
A reminder of those you love
Each time you hike the trails
To the mountain and rock above.

Always remember you are loved
Not just by those gone ahead,
But also by those who here remain
Whose names will stay unsaid.

And every time to you rest on Bald Rock
And think about life and its cares,
Just remember there is a Rock
Who each of your burdens will share.

As you rest fully on Jesus, our Rock
He will lift every care and woe
And you'll return from your special place
Refresh, renewed, and ready to go.

May this staff also remind you
Of the Great Shepherd who came
All of His sheep to care and keep,
He knows each of us by name.

~

Written with much love for
A very special woman—
Our daughter-in-love!

Levena Karr Hemmle
November 2016

So God made man in his own image, in the image of God created he him; male and female created he them. And God blessed them; and God said unto them, Be fruitful, and multiply, and replenish the earth, and subdue it...
Genesis 1:27–28

BIRTHDAYS ARE SPECIAL DAYS

Birthdays are special days
A time to remember and reflect.
A time to look back at all the ways
God has blessed your daily trek.

Some days were filled with joy,
While other days shed tears.
Some days there was sun to enjoy,
While other days you felt fear.

Regardless of the day-to-day ride,
There were constant treasures with you.
The love of your heavenly Father inside,
And the love of friends and family, too.

So armed with this love without and within,
You can face another year.
Knowing that whatever is around the bend,
You will not be alone in your tears.

A brand-new year is ahead of you,
A new year of blessings and gifts.
So don't be afraid or be blue
Receive this new year He gives.

Who knows what wonderful surprises
This new year has just ahead
For whatever challenge arises
There's no need to fear or dread.

You're not just getting older
For age is just a number, you see.
You're getting wiser and better,
So enjoy this year and be all you can be!

Levena Karr Hemmle
March 2007

And he said to them, "Come aside by yourselves to a deserted place and rest a while." For there were many coming and going, and they did not even have time to eat.
Mark 6:31

COME APART AND REST

Jesus said to "come apart and rest"
To a place of quiet and peace.
Where you can feel refreshed, renewed,
And a sense of tranquility.

So if even our Lord needed a time apart
To renew His inner self.
Then put aside your worries and cares,
Just lay them on a shelf.

And enjoy a special time all alone
Away from all the busyness.
Just let your worries melt away
With every gentle caress.

With some special pampering—
A refreshing massage to start.
Like Jesus, take a little time
For yourself to "come apart."

Levena Karr Hemmle
August 2011

Now unto him that is able to do exceeding abundantly above all that we ask or think, according to the power that worketh in us. Unto him be glory in the church by Christ Jesus throughout all ages, world without end. Amen.
Ephesians 3:20–21

GOD CAN TURN IT AROUND

God can turn it around
When sorrow and heartache abound.
Broken people and a broken world
Hide the treasure—God's great pearl.

Who can bring relief to life's woes
Is there not someone who sees and who knows—
The pain and suffering making your heart ache
The disappointments that make you break?

Yes, there is One who has felt your pain
The sting of betrayal—He's felt the same.
His heart, too, has been crushed and broken
Needing a word of comfort to be spoken.

Because He's been there where you are,
He knows what to do to heal the scars.
He has the power to overcome the pain.
He has the balm to soothe, heal the same.

His name is Jesus, Emmanuel, God with us.
He's Almighty God, the Beginning and First.
He can turn around every situation,
As we give Him our love and adoration.

He restores, refreshes, and renews
He will lead, guide, make dreams come true.
God can turn your present around
He can make your future really abound.

Your past is left behind you to forget,
No longer crippling, causing you to trip.
So never forget—listen to the sound
God is able and can turn it around.

Levena Karr Hemmle
January 2011

Grace and peace be multiplied unto you through the knowledge of God, and of Jesus our Lord.
2 Peter 1:2

HER NAME SAID IT ALL

A name can tell us much about a person,
Their temperament, character, or disposition.
Are they gentle or kind or loving,
Or hateful, bitter, mean, and uncaring.

My mom named Grace was a living example.
Her life and actions of God's grace a sample.
An angel smile and sparkling eyes of blue
And arms wide open to welcome you.

No one who ever visited our home ever felt
Any prejudice or coolness, for here God's love dwelt.
And how is that possible? you may ask.
It's because Mom and Dad looked beyond their past.

Grace was her name, and it filled her life
No one ever centered the door and stayed in strife
For they gave love and Southern hospitality
That soon dispelled any hostility.

Everyone left with more than they brought.
Something baked in her oven, rarely store-bought.
Usually a homemade pie or friendship cake.
A hand of love these goodies did make.

Yes, Grace lived up to her special name,
For it only described her with qualities of the same.
Gracious, loving, giving, and more describe
My mother's heart, where God did abide.

Levena Karr Hemmle
August 2010

In loving memory of my Mom, Grace, who lived the Proverbs 31 life before all who knew her.

How beautiful upon the mountains are the feet of him that bringeth good tidings, that publisheth peace; that bringeth good tidings of good, that publisheth salvation; that saith unto Zion, Thy God reigneth!
Isaiah 52:7

HOW BEAUTIFUL

How beautiful on the mountains
The feet that bring good news.
The voice that brings the message
From our bondage we are loosed.

How beautiful on the heads
The hands that touch with love
The arm of compassion reaching
To bring healing from above.

How beautiful on hearers' ears
The sounds of words of hope
The weary souls now uplifted
No longer rejection must cope.

How beautiful on beholders' eyes
The glory of His Presence
Hearts and souls touched within
His Spirit's renewing essence.

Not just my feet, head, and hand
I willingly give to You
But all of me, from head to toe,
For nothing less will do.

Levena Karr Hemmle
March 2008

Who can find a virtuous woman? for her price is far above rubies.
Proverbs 31:10-31

HYMN TO A GODLY MOTHER

The flutter of movement
within her being
A sure sign of new life
forming and beginning
What special purpose does
God have planned
For this tiny soul no bigger
than her hand?

For every child is unique
in their own special way
And each mother has her own part to play
In guiding and molding the pliable
heart and mind
To find and follow for her child
the Father's design.

She guides her children in the
way of the Lord
Setting the example first,
then seeing the reward.
Ever mindful of the cares and
desires of her little family
She rises early and lingers late to
meet those needs.

Willingly she toils with her heart
and her hands,
Unselfishly giving whatever
the task demands.
Be it clothing or food or matters of the heart,
She's always there to love and faithfully do her part.

As they sleep, cradled safe in
her arms against her breast,
She prays for God's peace and
love with gentle caress.
She asks for God's wisdom to
guide their little feet
In the way of righteousness,
and their souls to keep.

While they are young, filled with
insecurity and fears,
She cares for their scrapes and
kisses away their tears.
Then as they grow, new-found
 independence to try,
With wisdom and reassurance,
she gives them wings to fly.

All too soon the day of sorrowful
parting arrives.
She wonders, "Have I given
them the tools to survive?
This world where they are going
 can be very unkind,
Many pitfalls and snares and
traps they will find.

"But my task as their mother is never done,
For I know I can cover them in
the blood of God's Son.
He will protect them and keep
them from all harm,
And I know they'll surely be
safe in His strong arms."

They say a mother's job and
work is never through
And I, being also a mother,
have found this to be true.
For throughout life, from a
babe to a young woman or man,
Our influence is there, supporting and holding their hand.

Guiding, pouring out of our wellspring of compassion,
Into the image of Christ their young life to fashion.
So for wisdom from the heavenly Father above,
We pray and ask as we become extensions of His love.

Levena Karr Hemmle
May 2011

And call upon me in the day of trouble: I will deliver thee, and thou
shalt glorify me.
Psalm 50:15

LANDMARKS OR LAND MINES?

No one is exempt from hardship and trials
We all face difficult times
When it seems that we'll never again smile
Or experience a joy sublime.

These are times when we could go either way
In the valley low of dark depression
Or in the sunlight of a brand-new day
As we make a smile our daily expression.

Turning these land mines into a positive landmark
Means placing our faith and trust in God
Who knows how to give our lives a new spark
Of power and purpose as if from a lightning rod.

For land mines only bring death and destruction
To those found in the wake of their range
But landmarks become a hallowed reflection
Of victories won through the power of His name.

It's all up to you—don't be deceived or overtaken
By the land mines that come into your life
Instead, call on God, you'll not be forsaken,
Don't give in to the land mines and strife.

Turn them instead into places of victory
For God has promised His grace
Those land mines will become landmarks, you'll see
And instead of a frown, a smile will fill your face!

Levena Karr Hemmle
April 2007

That I may see the good of thy chosen, that I may rejoice in the gladness of thy nation, that I may glory with thine inheritance.
Psalm 106:5

A good man leaveth an inheritance to his children's children: and the wealth of the sinner is laid up for the just.
Proverbs 13:22

LEGACY OF LOVE

Today you're eight-two years young
And looking for more years beyond.
It's true you really don't look eighty-two,
I'm sure many wonder, "What do you do?"

I think your secret I have learned
It's part of your character, I discern,
Having a heart so willing to give
Determines how long a person may live.

An outstretched hand always reaching
To help those in need, broken and bleeding,
A kind word, smile, or a piece of candy
Are always ready, always handy.

Your life has taught us many truths,
A living example of true Christian proof,
Honesty, integrity, hardworking, and fair
Sharing and showing others that you care.

You've touched many lives, that's for sure.
Your faithful example has truly endured,
Lived out in the lives of those now touched
By the love of God, you've showed so much.

Thank you, Dad, for the bright reflection
Of God's great love and sweet affection,
Mirrored by your life through the years.
Today's a day for rejoicing—not tears.

Thank you, too, for your legacy of love
You've been a channel from God up above.
To follow in your steps is no small task
But to honor God, as you, is all we ask.

Happy Eighty-second Birthday, Dad!

Levena Karr Hemmle
March 2010

My little children, of whom I travail in birth again until Christ be formed in you.
Galatians 4:19

LET CHRIST BE FORMED IN ME

Father, let Christ, Your Son, be formed in me
His attributes and character let others see
Not for lauds nor praise of men
But for Your pleasure let me bend.

Father, let Christ, Your Son, be formed in me
A true reflection of Your love and purity.
May I walk in truth and in Your light
Leading those I meet out of this world's night.

Father, let Christ, Your Son, be formed in me
May I be an instrument always in key
From my life let Your anointing flow
So others may Your presence know.

Father, let Christ, Your Son, be formed in me
One in faith, one in purpose, one in unity
Let Your will for my life become known and real
As I kneel in Your presence, humbled and still.

Levena Karr Hemmle
November 2006

He appointed the moon for seasons: the sun knoweth his going down.
Psalm 104:19

And he changeth the times and the seasons.
Daniel 2:21

The heavens declare the glory of God; and the firmament sheweth his handywork.
Psalm 19:1

THE MASTER PAINTER

Brilliantly the trees share leaves of red and gold
Touched by the Master's brush of old
Hues of red, purple, orange, yellow, and green
Blended so perfectly—a breathtaking scene.

The Master Painter works His wonders of love
To give to us a canvas of color above
The fiery canopy of brilliant flame
Trees of summer green no longer the same.

The flame of fall will soon give way
To barren branches on a chilly day
In silent stillness, new life takes hold
First come the buds, then blossoms so bold.

Spring is a time of renewal and birth
For once again, His brush touches the earth
And colors of every tone and hue
Fill the landscape just for me and you.

Just as the Master Painter works on the earth
He wants to bring to us new birth
The fire of fall is as needful in me
As the stillness of winter for me to see.

That soon will come the rebirth of spring
And once again my soul will sing
Of His renewal and refreshing love
As I am touched by the Master Painter above.

Levena Karr Hemmle
November 2006

But if you return to me and carefully observe my commands, even though your exiles were banished to the farthest horizon, I will gather them from there and bring them to the place where I chose to have my name dwell.
Nehemiah 1:9

NEW HORIZONS

Leave behind the old and mundane
As we lift high Your holy name
Leave behind shadows of the past
As on Your Word we stand firm and fast.

Take us, Lord, to new horizons
Far beyond this world's toil and care
Let us see only Your precious Son
Lord, take us there, take us there.

New horizons bring a brand-new start
A new beginning, a bright new day
Renewed strength and refreshed heart
New direction to show me the way.

Levena Karr Hemmle
February 2007

But they that wait upon the LORD shall renew their strength; they shall mount up with wings as eagles; they shall run, and not be weary; and they shall walk, and not faint.

Isaiah 40:31

SOAR LIKE AN EAGLE

Lord, let me soar like the mighty eagle
Far above this world's toil and strife
High above the shadows dark
Renewed strength, renewed hope, renewed life.

As I wait in Your Presence, Your glory to see
Purge me and cleanse of all impurity
Remove the things that weigh me down
For only in You can peace truly be found.

Soaring high above clouds of doubt and fear
Baring my soul to You through my tears
Washed clean with clearer vision I see
The trials and tests sent were good for me.

Levena Karr Hemmle
April 2007

*Trust in the L*ORD *with all thine heart; and lean not to thine own understanding. In all thy ways acknowledge him, and he shall direct thy paths.*
Proverbs 3:5–6

THANK YOU, GOD

Thank You, God, for answered prayers
For all the ways You show You care.
For never saying, "I told you so,"
For friendships both new and old.

For giving me eagle wings to soar
For leading me through the open doors.
For giving me someone special to love
With a love that only comes from above.

Levena Karr Hemmle
July 2007

Then were there brought unto him little children, that he should put his hands on them, and pray: and the disciples rebuked them. But Jesus said, Suffer little children, and forbid them not, to come unto me: for of such is the kingdom of heaven. And he laid his hands on them.…

Matthew 19:13–15

WELCOME TO NEW BABY

There's a special bundle of joy very soon to appear
We've waited so long, can't wait till she's here.
It matters not the color of eyes or hair,
Olive skin like Mom, or Dad's skin so fair,
The thing that's important to know
Is that she's well and healthy, and so
With great anticipation we look for Savannah;
Both family and friends, but especially Grandpa and Nana.

Levena Karr Hemmle
January 1997

Written for my granddaughter's (Savannah Joy) baby shower.

I will give you shepherds who are loyal to me, and they will shepherd you with knowledge and skill.
Jeremiah 3:15

And when the chief Shepherd appears, you will receive the unfading crown of glory.
1 Peter 5:4

THE CHIEF SHEPHERD
AND THE UNDER-SHEPHERD

Called alongside, His voice softly beckons
Will you follow Me, My will to reckon?
Will you go to the dying, the blind, and the deaf,
Until it seems you've no earthly strength left?

Will you pay the price to find the lost and bleeding?
Listening intently, will you follow My leading?
Sometimes it will be on mountaintops high,
Your praise and joy will soar to the sky.

Still other times in the dark valley below
With the poor and hungry, their plight to know.
You'll weep and your heart will sorely ache,
To see the path they've chosen to take.

With My hand guiding yours, then take hold of the staff
Go lift them out and apply soothing salve,
To the wounds that have caused them so much pain.
Let them know of the peace they surely will gain.

To love and tend My sheep I have called you.
Not an easy task, but you must follow through.
For many sheep follow in your footsteps daily.
Keep your steps holy, keep them steady.

In return for your labor, you will know My strength.
My arm will lift you when your heart starts to sink
In the still of the night, My peace softly shines
To calm your heart and settle your mind.

My Word and the Spirit are the tools you will use,
Your rod and staff when the wolf's on the loose.
My under-shepherds you have now become
And I, the Chief Shepherd, till I call you home.

Levena Karr Hemmle
January 2006

And his sister stood afar off, to wit what would be done to him. And the daughter of Pharaoh came down to wash herself at the river; and her maidens walked along by the river's side; and when she saw the ark among the flags, she sent her maid to fetch it. And when she had opened it, she saw the child: and, behold, the babe wept. And she had compassion on him, and said, This is one of the Hebrews' children. Then said his sister to Pharaoh's daughter, Shall I go and call to thee a nurse of the Hebrew women, that she may nurse the child for thee? And Pharaoh's daughter said to her, Go. And the maid went and called the child's mother.
Exodus 2:4–8

LITTLE BROTHER

You've always been my little brother
Even though you're now a man
I wouldn't trade you for another
I hope this you understand.

You have a heart of gold, you see
Always willing to lend a hand
Even when you're busy as can be
You're always there to help if you can.

Your kind, gentle, and loving ways
Have endeared you to my heart
I loved you from the very first day
When on earth you made your start.

I tried to watch over you as we'd play
And keep you from danger and harm.
And when you got hit in the eye that day,
Crying, I carried you to Mom in my arms.

"His eyeball is gone!" I frantically exclaimed.
And ran back to the yard where we played to find it
I just knew for life you'd now be maimed,
Why did you get so close to the bat and get hit?

But Mom in her calm and loving way
Cleaned you all up till you looked brand-new
It was only a small cut—what can I say?
That had already started to close like glue.

Now you're all grown up with kids of your own
Two fine young men— Matthew and Sammy,
Both ready to leave the safety and comfort of home
A "chip off the block"—kind and loving like Daddy.

Many years have come and have gone
Lots of water has gone over the dam
You'll always have a place in my heart and home
No sister could be more proud than I am!

Levena Karr Hemmle
February 2007

Dedicated to my youngest brother, Steve. I was ten years old and he was
two when this incident took place.

Hear the voice of my supplications, when I cry unto thee, when I lift up my hands toward thy holy oracle.
Psalm 28:2

I will worship toward thy holy temple, and praise thy name for thy lovingkindness and for thy truth: for thou hast magnified thy word above all thy name.
Psalm 138:2

I will therefore that men pray every where, lifting up holy hands, without wrath and doubting.
1 Timothy 2:8

THE WORSHIP LEADER

With hands raised in sweet surrender
And face lifted toward the heavens above,
A glow of light in rays so tender
God's presence softly descends like a dove.

Into the very throne room of grace
He leads his people in boldness.
A chance to see God face-to-face
And witness His gentle forgiveness.

He breaks forth in a song of praise
A melody by angels inspired.
Our spirits to our heavenly Father raised
No longer downtrodden and tired.

Renewed faith and tender mercies
Are the results of his ministry,
As he beckons God's people to enter and see
Just how precious God's presence can be.

To deeper depths and a higher plane
He takes us on along the way,
Ever reaching further to obtain
Closer fellowship with God each day.

His ministry uses music and song
To proclaim God's Word, not as a preacher,
But after God's own heart to belong
Like David the Psalmist—the worship leader.

Levena Karr Hemmle
January 2006

Dedicated to two dear friends who are worship leaders now pastoring,
Rev. Gary Smith and Rev. Terrell L. Taylor

*For then must he often have suffered since the foundation of the world:
but now once in the end of the world hath he appeared to put away sin
by the sacrifice of himself.*
Hebrews 9:26

*Above when he said, Sacrifice and offering and burnt offerings and
offering for sin thou wouldest not, neither hadst pleasure therein; which
are offered by the law.*
Hebrews 10:8

*But this man, after he had offered one sacrifice for sins for ever, sat down
on the right hand of God.*
Hebrews 10:12

THEN AND THERE

Then and there, settled and done.
No more sacrifices needed to be made
Our sins and transgressions to atone
The perfect Lamb, His own blood gave.

Once and for all time and eternity
The price for our salvation was paid.
Jesus came to set at liberty
On Him our punishment was laid.

Then and there, on Golgotha's hill
He laid down his life for all
To fulfill and complete the Father's will
That we may be freed from Adam's fall.

Then and there, our healing obtained
By the stripes and torn, bleeding flesh
Of the spotless Lamb now slain
The wills of the Father and Son mesh.

Then and there, Satan was defeated
His evil plan had been halted.
When on the cross Christ was lifted
"King of the Jews," He was exalted.

Then and there, once and for all
He took the hands of God and man
And joining them together, we saw
Heaven and earth held by His pierced hands.

Then and there, my freedom was won
No longer was I bound by Satan's devices
The battle was won—it was settled and done
Because of His sacrifice, my heart now rejoices!

Levena Karr Hemmle
March 2007

And when they were come to the place, which is called Calvary, there they crucified him… Then said Jesus, Father, forgive them; for they know not what they do. And they parted his raiment, and cast lots.
Luke 23:33–34

He is not here, but is risen...
Luke 24:6

THE GREATEST EXPRESSION
OF LOVE

How do I love thee? Let me count the ways…
I left the splendor of heaven to spend with you my days.
I came as a newborn infant, born of lowly means
That I may learn from humanity, life is not always as it seems.

Though I left my home, where streets are paved with gold,
With beauty all around that place, the glory is still untold.
I came into a world full of trouble, strife, and envy,
And brought my Father's love and peace and joy to many.

With just a single word or touch of My outstretched hand,
Blind eyes and crippled limbs were healed at My command.
Loved ones were restored to life, or rescued from the angry sea.
I only wanted you to know, the great love I have for thee.

I sat at meals with you, and shared in your grief and joys.
I walked the same path, held in My arms your girls and boys.
I spent many days of teaching about My Father's love
I prayed for you, that you would receive strength from above.

After thirty-three years of life, My stay came to an end
For many did not understand how God could send,
His Spirit to a virgin maid who surrendered her all,
Much less acknowledge Me, or the "Son of God" call.

I was betrayed and falsely accused of blasphemy,
Endured a mock trial and beaten unmercifully.
Then forced to carry My cross in public shame,
I willingly went to Calvary and gladly bore the pain.

So you would know without a doubt or question
Just how much I love you, so you might know redemption.
How do I love thee? I counted many of the ways
So you could join Me in heaven to spend with Me your days.

With love unending,
Jesus

Levena Karr Hemmle
February 2009

But let it be the hidden man of the heart, in that which is not corruptible, even the ornament of a meek and quiet spirit, which is in the sight of God of great price.
1 Peter 3:4

Blessed are the meek: for they shall inherit the earth.
Matthew 5:5

MY BROTHER FRANK

My brother Frank was a gentle soul
Who was meek and humble in his ways.
As a child, he was never outgoing or bold
He preferred to play alone on many days.

Perhaps that was just a foreshadowing sign
Of the tragic path of his lonely life,
As illness plagued and gripped his mind
And robbed him of his marriage and wife.

Because Mom and Dad's strong faith was shown,
With the undying, unselfish love for their son.
The seeds of hope and healing were sown
Deep in the heart and mind of this dear one.

Sometimes in the middle of the dark night,
And other times in the middle of the day
He'd play the organ with all his might
Songs of heaven and Jesus—the only Way.

It seemed I was hearing the cry of his heart
To see Mom and other family gone on before
It gave me a reassuring peace in my heart
That he was longing for heaven's shore.

He fought his battle valiantly with the voices
That constantly seemed to torment and sneer
But today I truly believe he now rejoices
For he is reunited with loved ones dear.

So although we will miss his laugh and grin
I'm glad to know that he is finally free
Free from the bondage holding fast within
And again, someday, his smiling face I'll see.

I love you and miss you, Frank!

Levena Karr Hemmle
April 2010

Dedicated to my brother Frank, who is now with the Lord but who suffered as a paranoid schizophrenic as a young adult and the remainder of
his life—but a kinder, gentler, and softer-spoken person you'll never find.

In a moment, in the twinkling of an eye, at the last trump: for the trumpet shall sound, and the dead shall be raised incorruptible, and we shall be changed…. Therefore, my beloved brethren, be ye stedfast, unmoveable, always abounding in the work of the Lord, forasmuch as ye know that your labour is not in vain in the Lord.
1 Corinthians 15:52, 58

IN THE BLINK OF AN EYE

Ever notice how fast everything familiar to us can change?
Sometimes by something tragic or far-reaching,
Other times by something so small we can't imagine its range
Even reaching worldwide, causing such fear and fretting.

In the blink of an eye we can be standing before God
To give an account of our actions while here on earth
Searching and hoping for a "Well done, child" nod,
Which will come if we've experienced His new birth.

But what if we never took the time to turn to Him
And asked forgiveness, repenting of our sins?
"He won't forgive my sins, too many of them,"
We tell ourselves, "all I've done and the places I've been."

In the blink of an eye we'll be in His Presence
What a glorious reunion day for those who are ready
We'll see loved ones dear, smell heaven's sweet fragrance,
So keep your heart tuned upward and your walk steady.

It's not too late to make the change and turn to Jesus
He's always waiting with His hand outstretched to you
In the blink of an eye you can know this power of His
Life-changing salvation and love so true.

Levena Karr Hemmle
March 2020

I beseech you therefore, brethren, by the mercies of God, that ye present your bodies a living sacrifice, holy, acceptable unto God, which is your reasonable service.
Romans 12:1

And I myself also am persuaded of you, my brethren, that ye also are full of goodness, filled with all knowledge, able also to admonish one another.
Romans 15:14

RELATIVES OR RELATIONSHIPS?

Only an aunt can give hugs like your mother,
Can keep secrets like a sister, and share love like a friend.
Only an uncle understands a boy like no other,
Let you use his pocket knife, drive his truck in front of kin.

Only a cousin can be a best friend and know all your faults,
Know where your favorite hiding place is,
Roam through the countryside and find hidden vaults,
And if you found hidden treasure, oh, what bliss.

Families are a gift from God, they teach us to stay humble
While parents give us guidance and direction
It's our extended family that won't let us stumble
Because we tend to listen more to their instruction.

Sadly, not all families enjoy lives without sorrow
Divorce or death has changed our family structure
And we have to adjust and try not to borrow
The grief and heartache from our culture.

For those families who serve the Lord our God
Seem to enjoy more happiness and peace
Oh, they're not exempt from the negative nods
But they know the Source of true increase.

I urge you to have relationships, not just relatives
That include both family and dear friends
Because in them the love and joy that lives
Will last forever in memories that never end.

Levena Karr Hemmle
March 2020

And I said, Oh that I had wings like a dove! for then would I fly away,
and be at rest.
Psalm 55:6

HEAVEN'S MESSENGER

As my dad lay there in the hospital bed
We knew the end was near
When my daughter looked at me and said,
"There's a red bird sitting there."

My mom always loved her flowers and birds
Red birds were her favorite ones
We looked at the cardinal and knew for sure
Mom was there, Dad's journey now done.

For when we looked back to my dad
A big smile was on his face
And we knew we shouldn't be sad
For he had gone to a heavenly place.

A place where no sickness or pain
Could cripple or slow him down
For now heaven's joys he had gained
With Mom escorting him, no time to frown.

I've always heard that the little red birds
Were considered messengers from heaven.
I no longer think that it's so absurd,
The job the little red bird was given.

Levena Karr Hemmle
March 2020

Based on a true event.

And I saw the dead, small and great, stand before God; and the books were opened: and another book was opened, which is the book of life: and the dead were judged out of those things which were written in the books, according to their works.
Revelation 20:12

THE SCRAPBOOK

We all hold on to pictures, movie tickets, and mementos
Pieces of paper that hold special meaning to us.
Programs from special events, trinkets, or even logos
We don't want to lose, and if lost, we make a fuss.

We've packed away in shoeboxes special little items
Or perhaps we paste them in an album or big book;
They hold special meaning, we don't want to lose them
So they're tucked away till another day we want to look.

Reminds me of God's scrapbook that He is keeping
One for each of us until that special day
When He will open and reveal to us their meaning
And He will look at us and finally say…

"Well done, My child. You've been so faithful.
You've kept My Word and My commandments
Come, and enjoy this beautiful place so peaceful.
I've prepared a great feast and a robe of adornment."

But what if you're not in God's scrapbook? you ask.
He's kept a blank page just ready for you.
It's not too late on Him your worries to cast.
Just take a step toward Him—that's all you need do.

He's waiting and wanting to help you to fill
Your scrapbook with blessings and joys untold.
His hand's reaching out, He's waiting there still
To help you start filling your book, just be bold.

Levena Karr Hemmle
March 2020

In a moment, in the twinkling of an eye, at the last trump: for the trumpet shall sound, and the dead shall be raised incorruptible, and we shall be changed.
1 Corinthians 15:52

For our light affliction, which is but for a moment, worketh for us a far more exceeding and eternal weight of glory.
2 Corinthians 4:17

THE VALUE OF TIME

"How much time do you have?" we are often asked.
Enough to listen to friend who needs a listening ear?
We all have duties and chores with which we are tasked.
"Can't they wait another hour? I just need someone to hear."

"If only I had someone to talk to, someone who really cared."
Could your time given have prevented a tragedy?
True, there are just so many hours or days that can be shared,
But we never know how valuable our time if results we see.

So many milestones are attached to a certain time frame.
In nine months, we see the face of our newborn baby.
In milliseconds we see the Olympian who won his game.
In four years, parents rejoice with the graduate so happy.

One moment's hesitation at a crossroads or intersection
Can make a difference in someone's death or life.
The senior who failed his final exam and missed graduation.
Yes, time is valuable, my friend, don't fill it with strife.

Time waits for no one; it marches on with regard to none
It is not partial to wealth, or status, or even social standing
So treasure each moment you have with all your loved ones
One day you'll just have the memories, may they all be loving.

Levena Karr Hemmle
March 2020

Submitting yourselves one to another in the fear of God. Wives, submit yourselves unto your own husbands, as unto the Lord. For the husband is the head of the wife; even as Christ is the head of the church: and he is the savior of the body.... Husbands, love your wives, even as Christ also loved the church, and gave himself for it.
Ephesians 5:21–26

THE COUPLE'S BEATITUDES

Any day is a good time to express our love, usually with
  flowers or a card
Whether it's a first date or celebrating many years of marriage
To define what brings the years of success in a relation-
  ship is hard
It takes hard work from both the husband and wife, not
  to disparage.
In the dictionary the word *beatitude* is defined as "supreme
  happiness."
But what is the true source of that happiness? we may ask.
Is it wealth, or land, or beauty, or great items of worthiness?
To find the answer can become a time-consuming task.
I think the answer is found in God's written Word and
  commands,
Here are some suggestions you may consider when choosing
A life partner to be by your side that may help you understand
The importance of looking to the One who made you, it
can be confusing.

BLESSED or happy are they who love their mate
  more than any other person in the world they know
  and joyfully fulfill their vows of fidelity take,
  giving respect to one another always to show.

BLESSED or happy are those mates who forgive
  each other and make their home a place of rest.
BLESSED or happy are the husband and wife who live
  to be affectionate and considerate in spite of life's test.
BLESSED or happy are the husband and wife who are
  as polite and courteous to one another as they are to
  their friends.
After the wedding bells have ceased ringing, they've
  never lost sight of the love and joy they felt and
  vowed would never end.
BLESSED or happy are the husband and wife who faithfully
  attend the local church and together work for the Lord.
BLESSED or happy are the husband and wife who willfully
  work through problems with one mind and in one accord.
BLESSED or happy is the couple who understands
  that money is on loan from God to fulfill His purposes,
  keeping Him center.
BLESSED or happy are the husband and wife who
  humbly stand and dedicate their lives and home to
  Christ by loving all who enter.
BLESSED or happy are they who remember to thank God
  for their food and set aside time each day to read
  the Bible and pray.
Realizing the storms and trials of life and the road they trod
Will make them each stronger in their love every day.

Levena Karr Hemmle
March 2020

Beloved think it not strange concerning the fiery trial which is to try you, as though some strange thing happened unto you: Bu rejoice, inasmuch as ye are partakers of Christ's sufferings; that, when his glory shall be revealed, ye may be glad also with exceeding joy.
1 Peter 4:12–13

That the trial of your faith, being much more precious than of gold that perisheth, though it be tried with fire, might be found unto praise and honour and glory at the appearing of Jesus Christ.
1 Peter 1:7

FORGED BY FIRE

No one likes conflict or disagreements
Words are hastily spoken that hurt or damage
We'd much rather hear encouraging compliments
But it's all part of growing and maturing as we age.

These times of seemingly failures can be used for good
If we commit them to God and ask for His guidance.
Then the fiery trial that we experienced should
Burn out imperfections in our character and stance.

When we have come through the testing by fire
And all the dross and imperfections are gone
The things of this world we no longer desire
And only the gold of His Presence is shone.

So rejoice and be glad, dear friend of mine,
That you have been counted worthy for Him to suffer
Rejoice, look to Him, and let His glory shine
You conquered, withstood all the enemy's buffers.

Levena Karr Hemmle
March 2020

Wherefore seeing we also are compassed about with so great a cloud of witnesses, let us lay aside every weight, and the sin which doth so easily beset us, and let us run with patience the race that is set before us.
Hebrews 12:1

I have fought a good fight, I have finished my course, I have kept the faith.
2 Timothy 4:7

HOW ARE YOU RUNNING?

The shot rang out—the signal for the race to begin
"They're off!" the announcer cried over the speaker
Hearts were beating fast, the months of discipline
Had finally come for this athlete and dreamer.

Would the gold medal be his? Could he outrun the others?
In his mind he could see himself cross the finish line.
Had he trained well enough the others' effort to smother?
Would this finally be his moment in time to shine?

God has called each of His children to also run a race.
There will be times of hardship and difficulty.
We may even feel like giving up, a frown upon our face
But the training and testing is needed, you see.

To make us determined and strengthen our resolve
If we run half-hearted and don't give it our all
We'll surely fail, and our hope will dissolve,
And the next thing we know, we will then fall.

We must keep our focus on the finish line ahead
And determine, no matter what it takes to get there,
We're going to keep running and keep our stead
Keep your eyes on the goal and the winning share.

Reward comes to those who finish and cross the line
Though you may not be the first, you'll not be the last
For many are following in your steps and align
Their gait after you even in the shadow you cast.

Lead them to the finish line so all can rejoice
In finishing the race that was set before them
Receiving rewards for making the right choice
To run and finish the race of faith for Him.

Levena Karr Hemmle
March 2020

And desiring to be fed with the crumbs which fell from the rich man's table: moreover the dogs came and licked his sores.
Luke 16:21

DOG IS *GOD* SPELLED BACKWARD

I don't know about you, but I am an animal lover.
I especially love dogs for a number of reasons.
Not only are they warm and fluffy, but also a giver.
They're always ready to show love, no matter the season.

Now don't get me wrong, I mean no disrespect to God,
After all He's the One who made all the animals and pets,
So why shouldn't they have in them some of His good
But dogs have always been my favorite to get.

They are sensitive to our roller-coaster feelings and moods
And they're always ready with a tail wag and kissy lick.
Usually the more kids around make a really happy brood
Running and jumping with all—no favorite pick.

They can feel your joy as well as when you're in pain
And they snuggle close so you can feel their sympathy
Not looking for anything special to receive or gain
Anything more than your love and empathy.

Dogs love unconditionally, even if they're mistreated
That's the way God loves us, but even more deeply
He gave us His Son to die and be maltreated
Willingly He came, and on the cross died, not guilty.

So when my little dog snuggles close to me
I kinda feel like that's God drawing me to His side
Yes, unconditional love, trust, joy, and peace
It's like God came physically with me to abide.

Levena Karr Hemmle
March 2020

Dedicated to all my wonderful pets through the years. Many have crossed the Rainbow Bridge. We now have Emma Sue and Frankie. They are both dear to my heart!

*There shall not any man be able to stand before thee all the days of thy
life.… Be strong and of a good courage: for unto this people shalt thou
divide for an inheritance the land, which I have sware unto their fathers
to give them.*
Joshua 1:5–6

STAND STRONG AND TAKE COURAGE

Many oppositions come our way from day to day
Some are simple and easy to overcome or settle
But when the enemy of our soul tempts us to go astray
We must stand strong, take courage, and show our mettle.

Temptations come in many forms or the latest fashions
Sometimes it's substances that tempt to overindulge
Some are people or things, but all speak to our passions
We must stay alert and never our weaknesses divulge.

God knows us better than we even know ourselves
And He will help when we face the enemy's attack
He will lead us, and just as Jesus did for the twelve,
He'll help us be strong and know He has our back.

So be strong and of good courage each single day
Knowing you have the strength of God's army
Backing you up when the enemy comes your way
Take sword and shield, don't let fear alarm thee.

Levena Karr Hemmle
March 2020

...Be grave, not double-tongued, not given to much wine, not greedy of filthy lucre; holding the mystery of the faith in a pure conscience and let these also first be proved; then let them use the office of a deacon, being found blameless.... For they that have used the office of a deacon well purchase to themselves a good degree, and great boldness in the faith which is in Christ Jesus.
1 Timothy 3:7–10, 13

BE A MAN OF GOD

God is looking for men who will be strong and lead
Not only their household and their family
But also be an example to friends, ready to help a need
Whether related or in the church or community.

Be an example wherever you go, whatever you do
For you know others are watching your example
And hear the things you say, see the things you do
Always let the love of Christ in you be ample.

True, there's always struggles with the old ego
And temptations are everywhere you look
But the more of Christ's love you will show
The less the temptations can get a hook.

Keep the Word handy and always ready
To give an account of Christ's work in your life
Then your walk and your talk will always be steady
And you won't have to worry about the strife.

For the senses are the gateways to the mind
And Satan knows how to use and tempt them
Guard your eyes, ears, mouth, and find
You can escape whatever he sends.

Levena Karr Hemmle
March 2020

Dedicated to the men in my life—my husband, Rick; my son, Mike; my son-in-law, Kenny; my grandsons, Caleb and Graison, and my great-grandson, Micah; my brothers, Steve and Frank, and all my male nephews and cousins.

And Ruth said, Intreat me not to leave thee, or to return from following after thee: for whither thou goest, I will go; and where thou lodgest, I will lodge: thy people shall be my people, and thy God my God.
Ruth 1:16

THE LOVE OF A DAUGHTER

Daughters and daughters-in-love are special, indeed
Each one has their own unique talent or gift
Whether they are born from your seed
Or become part of your family, they give.

For me, I love them both the same degree
For each contributes in their own special way
The joy, laughter, corny jokes, or jubilee
That can make a difference in a normal day.

If you are blessed to have both in your family
And they both love and serve our God,
Rejoice and be exceedingly happy
For His blessings on you will be broad.

I'm blessed to have both a daughter-in-love and a daughter
They each bring their own unique joy and flavor
To our family events when we all gather
And the love we feel for each other, I truly do savor.

Their love and care for their husbands and family
Reflect in the love from those who have sown
Into their lives principles of love happily
So now to their daughters and sons are shown.

I couldn't be more proud of both my girls
I love them so much and always pray
That they will pass on to theirs the pearls
Of love and truth from which they'll never stray.

Levena Karr Hemmle
March 2020

Dedicated to my daughters, Kathy and Samantha.

Dew Drops and Honeycomb | 91

But seek ye first the kingdom of God, and his righteousness; and all these things shall be added unto you.
Matthew 6:33

LIFE'S JOURNEY TOGETHER

Congratulations to you both for your wonderful
   accomplishments!
Keep God at the forefront of your marriage so attitudes
   don't get bent,
Here are some tips to keep in mind, and your journey will
   be fun.
As you start life's journey together, two hearts function-
   ing as one,

One of you will need to keep a cool head to avoid conse-
   quences and backlash
Keep your mouth from spewing accusations, slander, and trash,
Never both be angry at the same time, especially when you
   hit the sack.
Once hurtful words are spoken, they can't be taken back.

"If you mess it up, then clean it up," your mothers prob-
   ably said.
Well, don't stop doing that just because you'll soon be wed.
Remember, every successful team must work together as one
Sharing chores, tasks, and responsibilities until they're all done.

Here's a tip to remember that gets folk in a lot of trouble
Keeping secrets from each other—your heartaches will double.
Be open and honest with one another and you will see
Your life will be filled with joy and sweet harmony.

Open all the windows of your heart, let the curtains be unfurled
Tell your partner you love them more than anything in
this world.
Do little things that make them happy, and show how much
you care,
Allow the refreshing of God's presence in your lives to be shared.

Before you know it, the day will come when you take each
other's hand,
But there will be times when you're tempted to remove the
golden band.
Remember you pledged to honor, cherish, and love for the
rest of your lives.
That unbroken circle of love and trust around your finger,
don't despise.

For the band of gold speaks loudly of your commitment
and your love
It tells others you belong to someone and your life is not
your own.
Dear Caleb and Regan, my prayer for you is that God's
heavenly Dove
Would sanctify and bless, flesh of His flesh, and bone of
His bone.

As you travel on your Life Journey together as man and wife
Remember to keep Him first in all your ways of living and life.
May God's Spirit go before you, open doors, and guide
your steps.
And He has promised to provide all your needs, His prom-
ise will be kept.

Love you both so very much,
Levena Karr Hemmle

Song and Chorus Lyrics

Sheet music available
upon written request to author/composer.

Title	© YR	Bible Reference	Key	Sheet Music Available
A Life Now Complete	2003	Eph 4:24; 2 Cor 5:17	F	Yes
All We Want	2001	Prov 3:5–6	F	Yes
Are You Ready?	2019	1 Cor 9:9–10		No
At Thy Word	2003	Luke 7:6–7	F	Yes
Because He Came	2009	John 12:46		
Before His Throne	2003	Ps 95:6	C	Yes
Come, Holy Spirit	2002	Acts 1:8	Bb	Yes
He Is Faithful	2001	1 Cor 1:9; 2 Thess 3:3	F	Yes
He Maketh No Mistake *	2002	See Note Below	F	Yes
His Manger Became His Cross	2009	Luke 2:7; Matt 27:54	F	
His Mercy Is Making Me Whole	2001	Psalm 136:23; 138:8		Yes
How Much More?	2009	Heb 9:14; Luke 12:28		
I Am the Lord	2007	Is 42:8; 43:15	F	
I Want to Lift You Up	2003	Ps 28:2	F	Yes
I'm Safe within His Arms	2001	Ps 18:2	F	Yes
It Takes the Same Blood	2008	1 John 1:7	F	Yes

Title	© YR	Bible Reference	Key	Sheet Music Available
It's All in the Blood	2007	Heb 9:22		Yes
Marching to Zion	2002	Rev 22:14	Bb	Yes
Mercy's Song	2002	Prov 21:21; Jer 33:11	F	Yes
Praises	2001	Rev 1:11, 18	D	Yes
Rekindle the Flame	2003	Ps 31:10	C	Yes
It Takes The Same Blood	2008	1 John 1:7	F	Yes
So Mysterious	2001	Eph 1:9; Col 2:2	C	Yes
The Great I AM	2001	Exod 3:14	F	Yes
The Lord Is My Strength	2002	Exod 15:2–3	F	Yes
The Riches of His Spirit	2001	John 12:1–8	F	Yes
Victory's Song	2003	1 Chron 29:11; Ps 98:1; 30:11	F	Yes
We Come	2009	Hebrews 9-13-14	F	Yes
Worthy the Lamb of God	2009	Rev 5:12	Ab	Yes
Wonderful, Glorious, Righteous	2008	Isaiah 9:6; 1 John 2:1	Ab	Yes
You Are Holy	2002	Ps 22:3; 145:21	F	Yes

* Poem/Lyrics He Maketh No Mistake Written by A.M. Overton; Music by Levena Karr Hemmle I didn't know if I could include the poem and lyrics since it was written by someone else.

Not sure if this poem has become public domain or not. Let me know what you think.

For if the blood of bulls and of goats, and the ashes of an heifer sprinkling the unclean sanctifieth to the purifying of the flesh; How much more shall the blood of Christ, who through the eternal Spirit offered himself without spot to God, purge your conscience from dead works to serve the living God?

Hebrews 9:13–14

WE COME

We will come into Your court in total surrender.
We will come into Your court in total surrender.
To lay before You our life on the altar.
To lay before You our life on the altar.
We will come into Your court in total surrender.

We will come into Your court in total surrender.
We will come into Your court in total surrender.
To lay before You our love and devotion.
To lay before You our love and devotion.
We will come into Your court in total surrender.

We will come into Your court in total surrender
We will come into Your court in total surrender
To lay before You our crowns forever.
To lay before You our crowns forever.
We will come into Your court in total surrender.

We come, we come, we come, we come

Levena Karr Hemmle
2009

For unto us a child is born, unto us a son is given: and the government shall be upon his shoulder: and his name shall be called Wonderful, Counsellor, The mighty God, The everlasting Father, The Prince of Peace.
Isaiah 9:6

My little children, these things write I unto you, that ye sin not. And if any man sin, we have an advocate with the Father, Jesus Christ the righteous:
1 John 2:1

WONDERFUL, GLORIOUS, RIGHTEOUS

Wonderful, Lord, to me You are so wonderful
You rain blessing down all over me
I am filled to overflowing.
Wonderful, Lord, to me You are so wonderful
Your tender mercies fill my hungry heart
I am touched by Your grace.

Glorious, Your love to me is glorious,
I surrender to Your sweet embrace,
For You make my life complete.
Glorious, Lord, to me Your love is glorious,
I'm surrounded by Your wings of peace,
I'm securely in Your love.

Righteousness, Lord, I hunger for Your righteousness,
To walk worthy in Your presence
And feel the comfort of Your grace.
Righteousness, Lord, I hunger for Your righteousness
Take my life and make it wholly Thine,
For my heart is set on Thee.

Levena Karr Hemmle
2008

For it is written in the law of Moses, Thou shalt not muzzle the mouth of the oz that treadeth out the corn. Doth God take care for oxen? Or saith he it altogether for our sakes? For our sakes, no doubt, this is written: that he that ploweth should plow in hope; and that he that thresheth in hope should be partaker of this hope.
1 Corinthians 9:9–10

ARE YOU READY?

Chorus:

Are you ready to put your hand to the plow
To work for the Master here and now?
Are you ready to surrender your mind and will?
To guard your tongue, keep it silent and still?
Are you determined to obey His sure command
To go and fulfill the tasks that He has planned?
Are you ready? Are you ready?

Verses:

We become settled and complacent
In our service to our Lord
Finding fault with those around us
Till our words cut like a sword.

Life's events and activities
Pull us away from His Church
We no longer yearn to be in His presence
For our hearts to be purged.

Don't put off renewing your vow
To live holy and faithful to God's call
Why continue in your half-hearted walk
Being a stumbling block to all?

Does your tongue speak words of
Peace and hope to all those around?
Do you long to once again feel
His presence, stand on holy ground?

Bridge or Chorus:

Ready to grow, ready to go
Ready to follow His sure command.
Ready to speak, ready to reach
Out to those in need with a helping hand.

Ready to sing, ready to speak
Of His mercy and grace so free.
Ready to give, ready to live
In His life abundantly.

Ready to go, ready to show
What His love will really do
Ready to talk, ready to walk
In His footsteps faithful and true.

Levena Karr Hemmle
2019

Trust in the LORD with all thine heart; and lean not unto thine own understanding. In all thy ways acknowledge him, and he shall direct thy paths.
Proverbs 3:5–6

ALL WE WANT

All we want is to worship You
For You are loving, kind, and true
You go before us in all that we do,
So all we want is to worship You.

Bridge:

We cannot place our trust in our own way
Our understanding's far too dim
But when we walk with You each day
We need not worry what's around the bend.

(Back to top)

Levena Karr Hemmle
2001

And that ye put on the new man, which after God is created in righteousness and true holiness.
Ephesians 4:24

Therefore if any man be in Christ, he is a new creature: old things are passed away; behold, all things are become new.
2 Corinthians 5:17

A LIFE NOW COMPLETE

Verses:

1. Wounded and broken, lonely and sad;
    looking for peace and feeling so bad.
"What are You teaching me, Lord? Help me see,
    my true inner self as You alone see me."
I yielded my will, my mind, and my soul.
"Come, Holy Spirit, cleanse and make me whole."

Chorus:

Beauty for ashes, truth for deceit
A life filled with love, a life now complete.
Joy beyond measure, and peace that's so sweet
A life filled with laughter, a life now complete.

2. Burn out impurity, in thought, word, and deed;
    I give You my all. Come, Spirit, and lead.
Back to His wounded feet, at the foot of the cross
    I surrender my life, I count it but loss
    To gain in return a life filled with glory
    To be once again, love's sweetest story.

3. No loss is too great to measure against;
    A life totally given, a life for Him spent.
My righteous rags pale, compared to His robe
Of purity and wholeness, covering my soul
For now in His beauty I stand all adorned
At peace and fulfilled, in Him fully reborn.

Levena Karr Hemmle
March 2003

Then Jesus went with them. And when he was now not far from the house, the centurion sent friends to him, saying unto him, Lord, trouble not thyself: for I am not worthy that thou shouldest enter under my roof: Wherefore neither thought I myself worthy to come unto thee: but say in a word, and my servant shall be healed.
Luke 7:6–7

AT THY WORD

At Thy Word, sick bodies are healed,
At Thy Word, empty nets are filled,
At Thy Word, broken homes are restored,
At Thy Word, weary spirits can soar.

Bridge:

At Thy Word, blind eyes see,
At Thy Word, the bound are freed
At Thy Word, the lame walk and the dumb can speak.
At Thy Word, the mountains melt
At Thy Word, Your love is felt
At Thy Word, I am changed evermore.

Levena Karr Hemmle
2003

O come, let us worship and bow down: let us kneel before the LORD
our maker.
Psalm 95:6

BEFORE HIS THRONE

When I kneel before His throne and yield
All my heart to Him alone,
Peace fills my heart, boundless joy He imparts
As I bow on bended knee.
His grace floods my soul like a mighty stream;
I'm bathed in His love, I have been redeemed.
No longer an outcast, new life I find
Cleansed and made righteous
Through Christ justified.
When I kneel before His throne and yield
All my heart to Him alone.

Levena Karr Hemmle
2003

But ye shall receive power after that the Holy Ghost is come upon you:
and ye shall be witnesses unto me both in Jerusalem, and in all Judaea,
and in Samaria, and unto the uttermost
part of the earth.
Acts 1:8

COME, HOLY SPIRIT

Chorus:

Come, Holy Spirit, come fill our thirsty hearts
        With Your power till they overflow
        With Living Water, fountain of blessing
        Spilling over to another soul.

Holy Spirit, descend upon us now   1.
with Your tongues of fire to purify.
Living Water, spring up within our hearts,
Let His holy name be glorified.

To this hungry world, we will go forth in joy   2.
Now empowered by God's holy dove.
Sharing Your good news of salvation's plan
Hungry hearts to fill with Your power and love.

Levena Karr Hemmle
2001

God is faithful, by whom ye were called unto the fellowship of his Son
Jesus Christ our Lord.
1 Corinthians 1:9

But the Lord is faithful, who shall stablish you, and keep you from evil.
2 Thessalonians 3:3

HE IS FAITHFUL

He is faithful, He is holy,
I will trust and serve Him only
Give Him honor, give Him glory
For He is faithful, holy, God.
I will praise Him in song
For He keeps me all day long.
He is faithful, He is holy,
I will trust and serve Him only
Give Him honor, give Him glory
For He is faithful, holy, God.

Bridge:

Feeling lonely and dismayed, I cried myself to sleep
Longing for the light of a new day, hoping His promises
He'd keep.
Yet deep within my heart I knew, He would not fail me now
Every Word He said is true, so at His throne I will bow.

Chorus:

He is faithful…

Levena Karr Hemmle
2001

Who remembered us in our low estate: for his mercy endureth for ever.
Psalm 136:23

The LORD will perfect that which concerneth me: thy mercy, O LORD,
endureth for ever: forsake not the works of thine own hands.
Psalm 138:8

HIS MERCY IS MAKING ME WHOLE

No matter how dark be my valley,   1.
No matter how deep my pit
His grace reaches past all my folly,
And takes me where my Lord does sit
There in His Presence nothing from Him dark or hidden
He shows me what I cannot see
My soul longing to be forgiven
His mercy is granted to me.

Chorus:

And it's higher than the heavens
And wider than my wand'rings
                His mercy flows over my soul
                Deeper than the pit of my sin,
Yet closer than my heartbeat
                His mercy is making me whole.

Eternal life, joy, and peace are now mine   2.
I rest in His promises each day
For grace brought me to His love divine
But mercy has opened up the way
How can I ever repay the debt I owe
To one Who has been so kind and true?
Each day He showers blessings from above
His mercy has filled me with His love.

Levena Karr Hemmle
2001

I am the LORD: that is my name: and my glory will I not give to another, neither my praise to graven images.... I am the LORD, your Holy One, the creator of Israel, your King.
Isaiah 42:8; 43:15

I AM THE LORD

I am the Lord, that is My name
And My glory I will not give to another.
Jehovah Olam, forever the same,
Wonderful, Counselor, Everlasting Father.

I am the Lord, the Holy One of Israel
I have redeemed you and called you by name
Lift high your praise, let the heavens fill
With your wonder and praises unrestrained.

Levena Karr Hemmle
2007

Hear the voice of my supplications, when I cry unto thee, when I lift up my hands toward thy holy oracle.
Psalm 28:2

I WANT TO LIFT YOU UP

I want to lift You up,
Lift high Your holy name.
I want to lift You up,
You're every day the same.

———

Your steadfast love surrounds me.
Your comfort and peace enfold me.
Your tender mercies renew me.
Your wondrous grace sustains me.

(Back to top)

Levena Karr Hemmle
2003

The LORD is my rock, and my fortress, and my deliverer; my God, my strength, in whom I will trust; my buckler, and the horn of my salvation, and my high tower.
Psalm 18:2

I'M SAFE WITHIN HIS ARMS

1.   The Lord is my fortress, in Him I can hide
He keeps me safe from danger as in Him I abide
The Lord is my Deliverer, from Satan's snares I'm freed
He's ever watchin' o'er me, I'll follow His sure lead.

Chorus:
He is my Rock and Refuge, I stand upon His Word
My shelter from life's storms, by His love I am assured
How can I trust another to keep me from all harm?
He holds my hand securely, I'm safe within His arms.

2.   He is my Strong Tower, to Him I can run
When Satan's forces threaten, the battle will be won
The Lord is my Defender, He's always by my side
I need not fear the trial, the vict'ry He'll provide.

Levena Karr Hemmle
2001

And almost all things are by the law purged with blood; and without shedding of blood is no remission.
Hebrews 9:22

IT'S ALL IN THE BLOOD

Crimson red flowed freely down,
Pools of scarlet lay on the ground,
Clouds of black hid the sun's face,
As the earth quaked at God's grace.

Yet God's innocent Lamb had died
His blood poured out—now crucified.
Sin's price had been finally paid
As on His back cruel stripes were laid.

Chorus:
Freedom from guilt, cleansing for sin
Healing for body and mind within.
Clothed in pure white, heaven's in sight
Because of Him—not by my own might.
For it's all in the blood.

Bridge:
Many men had hung there in shame
Guilty of crimes, another no name
But this man was different somehow
This One before whom every knee will bow.

Levena Karr Hemmle
2007

Blessed are they that do his commandments, that they may have right to the tree of life, and may enter in through the gates into the city.
Revelation 22:14

MARCHING TO ZION

Marching on to Zion's glory, with the saints to tell the story
How we conquered Satan's schemes and, lift our hands,
God's redeemed band.
Won't that be a glorious day, when forever with Him we'll stay?
Singing praises 'round His throne and basking in His love
all day long
How we'll thank Him for His mercy, all the sights and
wonder to see
Won't that be a grand and glorious day!

Chorus:
Singing praises, voices raised, and joyfully we'll clap our hands!
Thanking Christ for saving us and His redemption plan
With the saints of old to join 'round the throne to stay
Won't that be a grand and glorious day!

Levena Karr Hemmle
2002

He that followeth after righteousness and mercy findeth life, righteousness, and honour.
Proverbs 21:21

The voice of joy, and the voice of gladness, the voice of the bridegroom, and the voice of the bride, the voice of them that shall say, Praise the LORD of hosts: for the LORD is good; for his mercy endureth for ever: and of them that shall bring the sacrifice of praise into the house of the LORD. For I will cause to return the captivity of the land, as at the first, saith the LORD.
Jeremiah 33:11

MERCY'S SONG

I sing with joy, now I can see
Praise His name for He set me free
Free from the bonds that held me fast
Oh, praise His name I'm free at last.

No longer bound by sin's dread snare
I'm homeward bound to heaven fair
I'll live forever in His light,
I'll walk by faith and not by sight.

Bridge:
I have sweet peace no man can give
His blood has washed me clean
Now by His grace I am restored
Upon His Word I lean.

Now I can sing His mercy song
For to Him I now belong
And someday when this life is o'er
I'll sing His praise forevermore.

Levena Karr Hemmle
2002

I am Alpha and Omega, the first and the last...I am he that liveth, and was dead; and, behold, I am alive for evermore, Amen; and have the keys of hell and of death.
Revelation 1:11, 18

PRAISES

(D – F – Ab)

Praises, praises, praises to His name
Glory, honor, for He's every day the same.
Higher, lift Him higher; exalt Him on His throne.
Worship, come and worship, bow down to Him alone.

———

Earthly kings and powers, before Him will bow
Kingdoms and authorities surrender their pow'r
All creation trembles at the thunder of His shout
He plants His feet on the mountain,
the rocks and the hills cry out.

Praises... (F)

Choose this day which kingdom will hold your very soul
Let His pow'r flow o'er you, to cleanse and make you whole

Praises... (Ab)

Create in me a clean heart, O God; and renew a right spirit within me.
Psalm 51:10

REKINDLE THE FLAME

In deep contrition I kneel before Your throne
A fresh touch of heaven I seek.
Rekindle the flame of worship in me,
A greater passion for You I need.

Rekindle the flame, rekindle the flame
Rekindle the flame of worship in me.
Reveal more of Yourself in every part of my life
Burn out the sin and the strife.
A vessel of honor I long now to be.
Rekindle the flame of worship in me.

Levena Karr Hemmle
2003

Having made known unto us the mystery of his will, according to his good pleasure which he hath purposed in himself.
Ephesians 1:9

That their hearts might be comforted, being knit together in love, and unto all riches of the full assurance of understanding, to the acknowledgement of the mystery of God, and of the Father, and of Christ.
Colossians 2:2

SO MYSTERIOUS

So mysterious are Your ways, O Lord
So unsearchable, Your wondrous grace.
And I long to be in Your presence,
Humbly kneeling down before Your face.
Your tender mercies flow down from heaven's throne
To wash and to renew my weary soul.
I long for Your embrace of reassurance sweet
Filling my hungry heart, making me whole.

Levena Karr Hemmle
November 2001

And God said unto Moses, **I AM THAT I AM***: and he said, Thus shalt thou say unto the children of Israel,* **I AM** *hath sent me unto you.*
Exodus 3:14

THE GREAT I AM

Chorus: **
You don't have to kill the lamb anymore
You don't have to put the blood on the door
Someone has taken the place of that lamb,
He is the Great I Am.

He's the Bread of Life * that feeds my soul, *
The Door of the Sheep * protecting the fold *
The Light of the World * that guides my feet *
He's the Good Shepherd * providing my needs*
He's the Giver of Life, the Truth, and the Way
And in Him I'll always stay.

He's my Strong Tower * that I run into *
My Refuge and Strength, * the Rock I cling to *
He's my Shelter from the storm *
when the winds are blowing *
He's the Peacemaker * when the seas are rolling *
He's the Rose of Sharon on the mountain high
And the Lily of the Valley when I cry.

He's the Great Physician * when my body is ill *
He's the Baptizer, * my soul He will fill *
The Lion of Judah * and the King of kings *
He's the Morning Star * and the Song that I sing *
He's the Lord of lords, my life I give
And someday with Him I'll go to live.

He is the Great I Am, He's the Great I Am!

Levena Karr Hemmle
1994

Note: The * indicates that a choir should repeat "He's the Great I Am" after each phrase. **The chorus was originally heard as a Negro spiritual, composer of the chorus is unknown. Later I added the verses to emphasize who He is.

The LORD is my strength and song; and he is become my salvation: he is my God, and I will prepare him a habitation: my father's God, and I will exalt him. The LORD is a man of war: the LORD is his name.
Exodus 15:2–3

THE LORD IS MY STRENGTH

The Lord is my strength, He's my song and my salvation
He is my God, and my heart His habitation.
Naught shall I fear for He walks along beside me.
Holding my hand, safe in Him I shall be.
Him I exalt, He's forever the same.
The Great I AM, Lord Jehovah is His name.

Levena Karr Hemmle
2002

Then Jesus six days before the passover came to Bethany, where Lazarus
was which had been dead, whom he raised from the dead. There they made
him a supper; and Martha served: but Lazarus was one of them that sat
at the table with him. Then took Mary a pound of ointment of spikenard,
very costly, and anointed the feet of Jesus, and wiped his feet with her hair:
and the house was filled with the odour of the ointment. Then saith one of
his disciples, Judas Iscariot, Simon's son, which should betray him, Why
was not this ointment sold for three hundred pence, and given to the poor?
This he said, not that he cared for the poor; but because he was a thief,
and had the bag, and bare what was put therein. Then said Jesus, Let
her alone: against the day of my burying hath she kept this. For the poor
always ye have with you; but me ye have not always.
John 12:1–8

THE RICHES OF HIS SPIRIT

Wounded and broken she came
Nothing to lose, only sweet peace to gain
She poured out her precious treasure
From that moment she was never the same.

Chorus:
Life and peace came sweetly
As the Spirit drew her to His feet
She poured out her best
He gave her His rest
And the riches of the Spirit He gave freely.

No longer ashamed and broken,
She gladly shared the peace she had within
Those same riches can be mine
For His Spirit He freely will send.

Levena Karr Hemmle
2001

Thine, O LORD, is the greatness, and the power, and the glory, and the victory,
and the majesty: for all that is in the heaven and in the earth is thine; thine is
the kingdom, O LORD, and thou art exalted as head above all.
1 Chronicles 29:11

O sing unto the LORD a new song; for he hath done marvellous things:
his right hand, and his holy arm, hath gotten him the victory.
Psalm 98:1

Thou hast turned for me my mourning into dancing: thou hast put off my
sackcloth, and girded me with gladness.
Psalm 30:11

VICTORY'S SONG

I will praise His name, sing hosannas, sing, for He triumphs
 mightily.
I will praise His name, sing hosannas, sing, for His enemies
 all flee.
He wieldeth His sword o'er His head, and foes drop before
 Him as dead.
No power on earth can withstand the mighty anointing of
 His hand.

—

He is Jehovah, the God of power.
He holds the kingdoms of the earth in His hand.
He is Jehovah, the God of vict'ry.
He'll reign forever in this land.

—

I will celebrate, sing a new song, for the love He's shown to me.
I will celebrate, sing a new song, for His blood has set me free.
He took all my sins far away, and gives me sweet peace
 every day.
I'll praise Him with all of my heart and from His Word
 never more depart.

Oh, how I praise Him, how I adore Him.
My soul sings out a new song to Him.
Oh, how I praise Him, how I adore Him.
My soul sings a love song to Him.

Levena Karr Hemmle
2003

But thou art holy, O thou that inhabitest the praises of Israel.
Psalm 22:3

My mouth shall speak the praise of the LORD: and let all flesh bless his
holy name for ever and ever.
Psalm 145:21

YOU ARE HOLY

Holy, You are holy, holy is Your name
Righteous Son of David, and You're every day the same.
Perfect in Your wisdom, never failing Guide
Ever gently leading, and You're always by my side.
I will ever lift Your name in praise.
I will ever lift Your name in praise.
For You are my Lord, and You are holy.

Levena Karr Hemmle
2002

I am come a light into the world, that whosoever believeth on me should not abide in darkness.
John 12:46

BECAUSE HE CAME

I once was blind and bound by sin
My life a total mess
But Jesus came, brought peace within
I praise His faithfulness.
He gave me joy, a life brand-new
I sing a sweet melody.
His grace is mine, and His love is, too.
Now I live in harmony.

Chorus:

Because He came, now I will go
Because He came, His love I'll show
It was for me He gave His all
Now I will answer His love call.
Because He came!

Because He came, the grave has no grip
It has no pow'r over me.
Now I can live, since I took a dip
In Calvary's stream to see.
He conquered death to set me free
It cannot hold me down
Now I soar triumphantly
'Cause Christ rose from the ground.

Bridge:
Not for just a day or two
I'll give Him my whole life through
Come what may, life's trials and tests
Because He came, I'll conquer death.

Chorus:
Because He came, now I will go
Because He came, His love I'll show
It was for me He gave His all—O-o-o-h
Because He came! Because He came!

Levena K Hemmle and Terrell L Taylor
2009

How much more shall the blood of Christ, who through the eternal Spirit offered himself without spot to God, purge your conscience from dead works to serve the living God?
Hebrews 9:14

If then God so clothe the grass, which is to day in the field, and tomorrow is cast into the oven; how much more will he clothe you, O ye of little faith?
Luke 12:28

HOW MUCH MORE?

How much more will I break God's heart
Before I turn to Jesus, His Son?
How much more will I run from the truth
Knowing He is the only One, *Who can…*

Chorus 1:
Take my guilt and shame away
Give my life a brand-new day. *Only*
Christ can cleanse my heart and soul.
How much more, how much more?

How much more was Christ the perfect Lamb
Who laid down His life for you and me?
How much more did His blood satisfy
Took our burdens and set us free? *He can…*

Chorus 2:
Take your guilt and shame away
Give your life a brand-new day. *Only*
Christ can cleanse your heart and soul.
How much more, how much more?

Vamp:
The blood of animals could not satisfy.
That's why Jesus hung, bled, and died
He'll sanctify and satisfy your soul.
How much more, how much more?

Levena K Hemmle and Terrell L. Taylor
2009

And she brought forth her firstborn son, and wrapped him in swaddling clothes, and laid him in a manger; because there was no room for them in the inn.
Luke 2:7

Now when the centurion, and they that were with him, watching Jesus, saw the earthquake, and those things that were done, they feared greatly, saying, Truly this was the Son of God.
Matthew 27:54

HIS MANGER BECAME HIS CROSS

Verse 1:
See the babe, born in a manger
Created man, yet to many just a stranger.
Tears of joy, shepherds all around.
Who knew the day that this King would wear a crown?
Crown of thorns, and nails in His hands,
The day the manger became His cross.

Verse 2:
Hear the sound, a mother's gentle song
Love's lullaby, for her crying newborn Son.
The promised Seed, Messiah revealed
To take the pain, a broken world to heal
To set men free, for all eternity
The day the manger became His cross.

Chorus:
His manger became His cross
The Lamb sacrificed for the lost
He gave His life, the ultimate cost
The day the manger became His cross.

Verse 3:
See the tree that held His tiny frame
In swaddling clothes, so tenderly He lay,
Light of the world, Holy Lamb Divine,
Sin's sacrifice, by His Father's design
To redeem, and restore all things
The day the manger became His cross.

Levena K. Hemmle and Terrell L. Taylor
2009

Saying with a loud voice, Worthy is the Lamb that was slain to receive power, and riches, and wisdom, and strength, and honour, and glory, and blessing.
Revelation 5:12

WORTHY THE LAMB OF GOD

Worthy the Lamb who was slain for me
Worthy the Lamb who was slain for me
Worthy the Lamb who was slain for me
My life to Him I owe.

He took my place on Calvary's tree
He paid the debt to set me free
How can I give Him less than all?
Worthy the Lamb of God.

Worthy the Lamb of God,
Worthy the Lamb of God.
Praise and glory and honor we bring
Worthy the Lamb of God.

Levena K. Hemmle
2009

But if we walk in the light, as he is in the light, we have fellowship one with another, and the blood of Jesus Christ his Son cleanseth us from all sin.
1 John 1:7

IT TAKES THE SAME BLOOD

Chorus:
It takes the same blood to save all men
It takes the same blood, wherever you've been
No matter your nationality
His blood's good for all eternity
It takes the same blood, no matter time or space
It takes the same blood, to receive God's grace
His blood's good for all time and for all men.

Verse:
Whether good or bad, rich or poor
It's the same blood that gets us through the Door
It's not by works or deeds of good
It's not just living like I should
For the blood that cleanses the beggar's soul
Cleanses he who lives in a house of gold
It takes the same blood to cleanse and make us whole.

Bridge:
All I have to do is ask Him in,
Confess and He'll forgive my sin
Believe His holy, righteous name
Eternal life is mine to claim.

Levena K. Hemmle
2008

ACKNOWLEDGMENTS

- My children and their late father as well as my husband, who have encouraged me through the years to keep allowing the poems to flow;

- My pastors through the years who have inspired many of the poems within this work through their messages;

- And mostly my heavenly Father, who has loved me through so many difficult times. I cannot thank Him enough. My Lord and Savior, Jesus Christ, who has always been there for me, whispering words of encouragement. And the Holy Spirit, without whose anointing these would be just words on a page.

My prayer is that these writings would encourage and edify you as my brother and sister as well as the body of Christ..... "For the perfecting of the saints, for the work of the ministry, for the edifying of the body of Christ." Ephesians 4:12, 16

CPSIA information can be obtained
at www.ICGtesting.com
Printed in the USA
FSHW021641180720